mindset

in

motion

a guided journal

change your mindset – change your life

author

Jennifer S. Krencicki, MS, LPC, BCC

editorial & creative partner

Katelyn Gore

For My Boys,

May you always have a Mindset

that Serves you Well.

interactive playlist

This journal was created in tandem with audios and videos to accompany certain days and activities in order to help guide you on your path toward reaching your goals. While one day may have an encouraging word from our author, another may have a guided meditation for you to utilize as a part of your day's activity.

Below you will find a unique QR code that brings you to this private interactive playlist. Each time you see the ' ▶ ' symbol, scan this QR code using your cell phone's camera and find the video with the corresponding title.

Enjoy your journey!

table of contents

part one:

Setting Up for Success

introduction

We are all a Work in Progress...Always!

And when it comes to Embarking on your next Change Journey, Mindset is Everything.

Change is the only Constant. Everything changes, as it should. Ironically, for many of us, change is difficult and scary. As a result, we remain in many places, situations, and in conditions of body and mind that are unwell. We stay in comfortable places within ourselves and in our surroundings because, even though it makes us unhappy, it is familiar. And if those comfortable places are working out for you, wonderful! But sometimes (many times) those comfort zones, of self and life, are getting in the way of what we actually want for ourselves. So, we set out on a journey to change. We make resolutions and get all the things needed to get started (daily planners, fruit and veggies, exercise bands, organizers, etc.). And then we rock it out… for a few days, maybe a week or even two. Then we yo-yo back to the compulsions of habit that are more aligned with our origination than with our destination.

What is Mindset, and Why Does It Matter?

Every day of our lives, we have had neural activity going on that has given us a way of relating to the world around us. We experience this neural activity as thoughts. The thoughts then tell us what meaning to make of the situations and experiences that we have throughout the day. When we are small, these thoughts are largely governed by our feelings combined with only limited knowledge and information. While we are still working out the details during this time of our life, we attach specific thoughts to specific experiences, and patterns evolve. We begin to develop beliefs based on these thoughts and feelings. The beliefs then shape our perception about the world around us and our place in it. The more we invest, or buy stock, in these beliefs, the more they produce the same. Beliefs turn into larger schemas, and what is created in your mind is a set of ideas, knowledge, understandings, and beliefs about self and life. This becomes your mindset. Your mindset tells you things from this schema like, "I can do this!", or "I can't do this!"; "This is hard", or "This challenge is exciting". This message shapes the choices that you make, the actions that you take, and influences your whole lifestyle.

Let's say something or someone told you early on that you are not lucky, and you start to believe it. You go about life with this base knowledge that you are an unlucky person. There is a good chance you will skew any information that might tell you otherwise because it does not fit with who you have understood yourself to be. You play games of chance half heartedly and even cautiously or anxiously because you are sure you will lose. And if you are okay with being unlucky, then it does no harm to continue that storyline. But if one day you begin to think, "I wish I was one of those lucky people", then that unlucky mindset is not going to serve you any longer. Each time you try to be "lucky", your beliefs will get in the way. Your mindset has to be aligned with what you are desiring in order for it to be. Otherwise, all sorts of unconscious psychological, emotional, energetic, and even physical barriers will present themselves.

To sum it up, before any change can happen and stick, Your Mind has to be ready for it. So, let's get to it.

before you get started

You're Invited ▸

Dear Change Seeker,

Welcome to this 19 Day Mindset Journey. This guided journal is for ANYONE who seeks some type of change. Whether you want to get healthier, improve your career, have a better social life, have a different quality of life, or simply just want to feel happier and less stressed, the change you seek will start and continue with a Mindset that promotes and maintains the incremental adjustments that are necessary to get to the goal.

In this journal book, there is an entry for each day that invites you to participate in Mindfulness and Mindset exercises and activities. These are designed to promote an overall Mindset practice that applies to all. Please personalize each practice to relate and apply to your specific situation, needs, goals, and desires.

As with all things, you will get out of this journal what you put into it. I strongly encourage the following to really get the most out of this experience:

-Set aside enough time each morning (before you start the day) to read through the day's concepts and exercises. Some of the exercises will require dedicated time and you will want to plan for it to be successful. You will notice each day will invite you to take time for an Evening, and/or Morning practice in addition to the day's themed concept, journal activity, and mindset practice.

-I encourage you not to move on to the following Day until the Day you are in is completed. Each day is sequential, and this is a process that builds as you go. Even if you miss a day, just pick back up at the point where you left off. Let this be a promise you make to yourself to complete each day (before you move on) even if it takes you longer than 19 days to complete.

-If you feel unprepared to follow through with any one Day in the journal, that is OK. Things happen; Life happens. Take a pause for a day and come back to the journal when you feel ready to resume with effort. If you do a day through but realize you only did it "half-way" or wanted to give it more of your attention, pause and do it over tomorrow before you move on.

*-Lastly remember, this is <u>YOUR JOURNAL</u>. As such, you will find a space for personal reflection each day. Let this be **Your** Journey toward the Mindset that will Serve you best. And with that, make yourself a promise to invest your time, attention, and energy into it.*

*-Be Accountable to this Promise that you have made to yourself and **Enjoy Your Journey!***

JSK

8

day one
"Visioning"

If what you are doing right now is working for you, keep doing it.

If something isn't working out for you, it's time to change it and find what works better.

These first few days are about seeing the "You" you want to be and gaining greater self- awareness on the "You" you are today. We are ever evolving, complex creatures. You are not all one thing or another. You have traveled along a path from the time you came into this life. Where you are today is a point on that road, and you have done many things already to get yourself here. This is a journey about furthering that road towards a destination/future you seek. It is important to get a crystal-clear picture of what you want to see as your reality in the future. Where are you trying to get to? What do you want to see there? When you are there and you look in the mirror, who do you want to see? What do you want to be hearing in your own mind that day?

This practice is called Visioning. Visioning is extremely important in this process. It sets the mark for what you are about to do next. It is simply planning your trip's destination. Most of us do exactly that when we decide to take a vacation or trip somewhere. Occasionally we may plan a "let's see where we end up" type of trip. But for the most part, we select a destination based on what we think it will be like- the fun we will have, the gorgeous weather or sights we will see, the experiences we want to have there. We have images through brochures, website pictures, and the images we create in our own minds about it. We see ourselves there and we think about it again and again with excitement leading up to the day when we can finally get there. This Visioning is just the same. You will decide on the destination and invest in what that will look like. But not to worry, this is not a fixed process, so if this journey happens to take you to a new destination that you hadn't planned for- that's ok too.

Today you will spend as much time as you can throughout the day creating your Ideal Picture in your own mind. Use the Day One- <u>Visioning Journal</u>

<u>Activity</u>to get the image out on paper. This makes it "real," as you see it in print or drawing. Here you will describe in words or pictures your Ideal for yourself. Be specific: what do you see around you and in the mirror, where are you, what are you doing, who is with you (who is not), what is the quality of your health and life, and so on- every little detail you can imagine. Add to it throughout the day whenever you can, or simply reflect on the picture when the moment allows.

Give yourself an extra 10 minutes before you go to sleep tonight. Get comfortable, lie down in your bed, close your eyes, get ready to shift out of your conscious mind state, and "dream". See the picture that you have designed all day long. Invest in this Vision, give it your time, your mental focus, and your belief. Let yourself bask in the vision, let yourself feel all the feelings that come with it. Take all the images, sounds, and feelings with you into your nightly rest and your unconscious experience.

<u>Day One- Mindset Journal Activity:</u>

Creating and Practicing Your Vision

Use this journal page to write, or even draw, the details of your Ideal Self that you are envisioning. You can daydream away and paint a picture of yourself having met your long-term goals. Or you can get an image of yourself a week from now, a month from now, at the end of this journey, etc. You decide how far out you want to see yourself and what that Ideal version of you looks like at that time. Describe through your senses: what do you see, hear and feel here?

space for reflection

day two
"You Are Here"

From Explorer to Navigator ▶

Welcome to Day 2. I hope you had a blissful night's sleep priming yourself for transformation. Now that you have associated the sensory experiences (see, hear, feel) with your personal Destination on your change journey, we will need to assess the best route to get there.

Now if you were heading toward Ft. Lauderdale from Philadelphia, you wouldn't map a route starting in Baltimore, right? Nor can you determine the sequence of steps toward the change destination in your own life with a starting point that is inaccurate, or simply put, "not where you currently are".

So today is about really getting to know yourself, as you are right now. Without scrutiny or judgment!

This exercise is not about regret or criticism about where you are, where you aren't, or how you got here. It is about honestly assessing what your starting point is. Think of it as the pinpointing that, "You Are Here," symbol on the map at the mall. Sometimes it takes a minute to figure out where you are on that map, but once you do, you can almost hear yourself say, "Oh Okay, here I am. So that means I need to go this way." Knowing your true starting point empowers you to know what your realistic next steps will be. This is extremely important, because (back to our road map metaphor) if you start your journey with the map from Baltimore instead of Philadelphia, you will be lost for about 100 miles. When we feel lost, we are more likely to quit. If the leap is too big from our current habits of thought and behavior to the habits that we are trying to implement, the same is likely to happen.

Our habits have a starting point (a cause or reaction to an initial life circumstance or event). But over time, they simply become Habits-something that feels "right" or natural to us, so we continue to do it. After enough time of doing certain things, and thinking a certain way, it feels so comfortable that it becomes something that we are just compelled to do always. Some of these habits are working for you; some may not be. Let this be your Origination Point on the next part of your life journey and personal evolution. You have walked a long road

20

already that has led you to this place, this moment. You surely have had many challenges, bumpy roads, detours, and potholes along the way. You likely also had some smooth roads, beautiful scenery, and straight paths too. It is all GOOD. There is nothing to regret, nothing to look down upon, nothing to feel shame for. It has ALL been a part of where you are right now, and where you are about to Go.

Today's exercise is all about Self-Acceptance. It is about empowerment through getting to know yourself and defining your starting point on this journey toward your 'Ideal You'. Use the <u>Day Two- Self-Inventory Journal Activity</u> as a tool to help you get to know yourself a little better by keeping track of your Habits of Thought and Action throughout the day.

In addition to today's exercise:

1.) Continue to give yourself moments of mindfulness (or what we will call, "Mindful Moments," throughout this journal) of your Ideal Self-Vision that you created on Day One.
2.) Set aside 10 minutes this evening to Reflect on today's journal entry. Look for trends and relationships between your Habits of Behavior, Thought, Eating, Movement, and Mood. There

are reasons that these habits came to be, and you most likely know where they come from and why they stuck.

<u>Evening Reflection</u>: *Revisit, Reflect, Relax* ▶

3.) *Close your eyes and see yourself as you are right now. Just as you are. And as a mother or father would see their child, look at yourself with unconditional love and acceptance. Honor the road behind you; give yourself Compassion for the Challenges you have traveled through and revisit the beautiful sights along the way. Appreciate the point on the map that you stand on today and know your ability to go the distance beyond.*

4.) ***Evening Mindset Practice:*** Take 5-10 minutes before bed to do your Visioning practice (from Day 1). Find a comfortable place to sit or lie in bed before you go off to sleep, and let your mind go to that place of Your Vision. (We will continue each day with an Evening Mindset Practice similar to today's, yet slightly tailored at times to the day's exercise).

Day Two- Mindset Journal Activity:

Self-Inventory

Today you will do everything as you typically do in your usual routine and habit. Do not change ANYTHING! Just pay attention to what it is that you are doing and thinking. Use this journal entry to collect those thoughts and actions as you go through the day.

The first thought I had when I woke up this morning was...

____

____

____

____

My next 3 Actions and Thoughts of this day were...

Action: ____

____

Thought: ____

____

Action: ____

Thought: ______________________________________

Action: ______________________________________

Thought: ______________________________________

How do I feel on this day?
Physically, Mentally, Emotionally?

For the remainder of your active day, pay close attention and use the template on the following few pages to log your Habits of Behavior, Thought, Eating, Movement, and Mood. If possible, keep it on hand to log as it occurs throughout the day, or take breaks and reflect.

Habits of ***Behavior***:	■ __________________________ ■ __________________________ ■ __________________________ ■ __________________________ ■ __________________________
Habits of ***Thought***:	■ __________________________ ■ __________________________ ■ __________________________ ■ __________________________ ■ __________________________
Habits of ***Eating***:	■ __________________________ ■ __________________________ ■ __________________________

Habits of **Eating** (Continued):	▪ ________________________________ ▪ ________________________________
Habits of **Movement**:	▪ ________________________________ ▪ ________________________________ ▪ ________________________________ ▪ ________________________________ ▪ ________________________________
Habits of **Mood**:	▪ ________________________________ ▪ ________________________________ ▪ ________________________________ ▪ ________________________________ ▪ ________________________________

Heads up, you'll be reflecting on this page tomorrow.

space for reflection

day three
"Bridging the Gap"

The Path to Lasting Change ▶

Regardless of what change you seek; Sustainable Change comes from Incremental Change. Whether you desire better health, more money, confidence, a more fulfilling career, etc., there will be a series of small steps that get you there. That is not to say big, dramatic change is not possible. Big, unexpected changes happen all the time; some welcome, some not so much. And sometimes we are forced to dramatically re-adjust, whether we like it or not. But without a forced change event, Sustainable Change (change that sticks) is most successful when we do it slowly over time. We gradually create for ourselves a New Normal with new habits of thought and action and give ourselves time to allow those new habits to feel natural enough to sustain themselves. Too often, we go from zero to 100, only to go back to zero (sometimes below).

Today's exercises are about the Comparison between your Ideal Self Vision and your Self Now Inventory. As if you could overlay a transparency of your Self Now over your Self Vision, today is about identifying where the gaps are and determining the first steps to create your bridge. You will use the <u>Day Three- 'Bridging the Gap' Journal Activity</u> to guide you along the exploration and identify next steps.

<u>Evening Reflection:</u> *"Wiring In" Your Ideal Self* ▸

In addition to your journal entry, take time today to mentally embrace the process of Getting Ready for Change. Offer yourself a time at some point in this day to formally meditate on your Day 1 Ideal Self Vision. It is necessary to wire this into your neural network. Create a space that is quiet, private, and uninterrupted. Get comfortable in a seated or lying down position. Close your eyes and breathe. Notice the breath coming in and out through your nostrils. With each breath, let the picture in your mind's eye of your Ideal Self get clearer and more vivid. Each time any other thought floats in, let it float back out through your breath and come back to the Vision. If you hear a sound outside or nearby, breathe and tune into the sounds where you are in your Ideal Self Vision. Maybe even hear the words you are saying to yourself there. If you feel any physical sensation, breathe, and return to your

Vision, feeling what it feels like to be there. Spend as much time as you can in this meditative space connecting your neural pathways to this new reality. When you are ready, open your eyes and return to your day or rest until tomorrow taking this experience with you.

Evening Mindset Practice: Either do the <u>Day Three Evening Reflection</u> right before bedtime or take 5 minutes to reflect on this exercise while lying in bed just before you fall off to sleep.

<u>Day Three- Mindset Journal Activity</u>:
Bridging the Gap

Go back to your Ideal Self Vision / Day One journal entry. Look at the words and images on the page. Now close your eyes, and step into the image of yourself on that page. Get a clear and focused picture of all that you will be, do, have, think, and feel there. Ask your Ideal Self to turn around and see the path that you followed from your 'Self Now' to where you are there. Answer this question from the perspective of your future Ideal Self:

What steps did you take to get from where you were to the Ideal Self you are now?

____

____

____

____

To help you in answering this question, lay out before you your Vision Exercise (Day1) and your 'Self Now' Inventory (Day 2). Looking at the journal pages side by side, what stands out to you as your starting point, your one next step forward?

Use a highlighter, crayon, colored marker, or something that grabs your attention, and highlight or circle the item or items that you know you are ready to "Level Up" toward change.

Write down the very first steps that you will take to get on the path to your Ideal Self:

1.____

2.____

3.____

Free Write: Use this space to freely journal any thoughts, reactions, awareness, or challenges during the first three days of "Getting Ready for Change":

____

____

____

____

____

____

day four
"See It to Believe It"

Practice Makes Progress ▶

Mindset is Everything. What your mind tells you is what you will do, what you will be, what you will feel. Mindset is not Magic. This is not about willing something into being while sitting on the sidelines just waiting for it to fall out the sky. But Mindset *will* determine whether or not your choices align with your goals. So, before we DO anything, we need to know what and how to THINK about it. We must consciously give our minds the information/data it needs to promote new choices.

To do this, we must create or activate new neural pathways in our brains-new roads to success that your mind can see, hear, taste, smell, and feel. In this way, you will be creating a reality in your perception that gives you the room and the ability to try on new behaviors. This is an example of priming your mind for the desired action and change that you are setting in motion. You must create the reality in your mind before you can successfully create it in your life. Otherwise, attempts at new behaviors, thought choices, and habits will likely be rejected or resisted. There may be multiple reasons why this is, but for now let's focus on how to move forward with opening pathways in your mind that will allow good changes to begin.

Today, we are going to borrow a technique from Motivational Interviewing known as "The Miracle Question". We will adapt it a bit for our purposes.

In the 'Getting Ready' phase, you were able to identify your first next steps toward the change you desire. That change might be how you feel, how you think, your life situation, or all the above.

Now imagine that when you go to sleep tonight, a miracle occurs, and you wake up tomorrow in that exact reality. Everything you desire in yourself and in your life-experience is achieved.

Use the <u>Day Four- 'See It to Believe It' Journal Activity</u> to describe what you see, hear, think, and feel.

Evening Mindset Practice: Take at least 10 minutes before bedtime to do your Visioning practice. Again, YOU decide how far out you want to create your Vision. You can practice Visioning for a year from now, or maybe just even for the next day. Plan for this (or a version of this) to be a daily activity. Let this become a new Mindset habit.

<u>Day Four- Mindset Journal Activity</u>:

See It to Believe It

Let's use the premise of The Miracle Question, a tool from Motivational Interviewing, to allow our neural network to activate around the specific details of the change we want. Imagine that miracle occurs while you are sleeping tonight. When you wake up tomorrow morning, the change that you are looking for has happened. Answer the following questions. *Be specific as this information will be used for more Priming as we go forward.*

What is the very first thing you notice when you wake?

____

____

____

____

Where are you? Who is there?

____

____

What are the sights, sounds, smells, and feels you
notice?

____

____

____

____

What do you notice at first glance when you see
yourself in the mirror?

____

____

____

____

What do you feel in your body?

____

____

____

____

What do you hear yourself saying in your own mind?

____

____

____

____

space for reflection

day five
"Time to Prime"

Priming Your Mind for Change ▶

As with anything, Consistency is key. You have had a
lifetime up until now to develop your thought habits.
You have been practicing these habits every day
consciously, and then ultimately, unconsciously. We are
bringing those unconscious habits to the conscious mind
so that they can be broadened, expanded, and changed.
We began this expansion yesterday with creating new
neural pathways by seeing the possibility of your new
personal narrative. The goal today is to activate this new
neural data points in your brain activity as much as
possible so that the network is lighting up in there. This
is how we Prime our Minds for what we want, instead
of focusing on what we don't want.

So today you will be simply practicing your new
narrative. You will do this by reflecting on your

responses to the Miracle Question from yesterday and your <u>Day Four Journal</u> entry. Take this information with you wherever you go today. You can either take out your journal page or rewrite each response down on a separate index card, sticky note, piece of paper, or notepad entry on your phone.

Carry your notes with you throughout the day and select moments (all you need is 30-60 seconds for each) to insert any one of those given thoughts, feelings, visions, smells, tastes, etc.

If a particular image, sound, or sensation is not present or accessible in the environment, close your eyes and travel to a place internally where you can see, hear, smell, taste, or feel it through your memory.

Set a goal of doing this activity a minimum of 3 times today. If you want to do more, go for it! There is no limitation on creating new pathways in the mind.

Really let yourself enjoy this practice!

It can be 30 seconds of delight in your day. 60 seconds of transformation in the making. Breathe in the good thoughts and feelings that come with this practice each time you exercise it. Let it be a shift out of something unwanted or bothersome that is happening, if needed. Pay close attention to how it feels to let yourself be in brief pleasurable moments. Write freely using the <u>Day</u>

<u>Five-Priming Journal Activity</u>to really acknowledge and reflect on these moments. We will use this data first thing tomorrow with a Morning Exercise.

<u>Evening Reflection</u>: *Reset & Revisit* ▸

Evening Mindset Practice: Keep up with your new nighttime habit of taking 10 minutes to do your Big Picture Visioning!

Note: Be prepared to give yourself an extra 5-10 minutes tomorrow morning before you really get into your day.

<u>Day Five- Mindset Journal Activity:</u>

Priming for Change

Free Write/ Reflection: Use these pages to reflect on your experience today with Priming. Describe on anything that felt different today as you continued to purposely activate information in your brain that allowed you to see yourself in a new way.

space for reflection

day six
"Setting Your Intentions"

So often we just wake up and run and gun into the day. Don't self-judge: We ALL do it!

Developing a Mindset Practice also involves building Mindfulness. We are learning how to course-correct the robotic-like patterns that set us up for reactive (instead of responsive) habits of living.

It all starts with the moment your conscious mind enters the day. We build mindfulness through awareness and use that mindfulness to make choices—choices of thought, and ultimately, behavior. You are creating a daily experience in which You are the designer. Not by waving a magic wand and *thinking* it into being, but by intentionally positioning yourself in the situations of the day in a way that will serve you. Think of it as optimizing the day you are about to have, **stepping into**

your day with Purpose. - (not Problem or Perfection). A morning ritual of Setting your Intentions for your day promotes Mindfulness right at the Start (before getting distracted by the hundred things waiting for you). This is your opportunity to **Prime your Mind** for the day in front of you. Use today's <u>Affirmation Exercise</u> on the next page to give you jumping-off point for creating a new morning ritual of Intention Setting.

<u>Day Six Mindset Priming / Affirmation Exercise</u>

Find a time and a space in which you can focus your attention and intention. Take 3 deep belly breaths in and out for grounding your body and mind. Read the statements below either quietly to yourself or aloud. Create Intentions for your thoughts, words, and choices. When finished the Affirmation Exercise, use the <u>Day Six- 'Daily Intentions' Journal Activity</u> to formalize this practice with written statements that you will set in the morning and hold yourself accountable to in the evening.

<u>Mindset Practice</u>
Affirmation Meditation ▶

I AM Present to This Day of My Life.

I AM Grateful to have this day of Opportunity.

I CAN be aware of my thoughts and reactions to the events of this day.

I AM capable of making choices in this Day that will serve me Well.

I enter this Day with Purpose.

Evening Mindset Practice: Using your journal entry to assist you, reflect on the Promises that you made to yourself at the start of this day. Without judgment, notice what promises you fulfilled. If something stands out as room for progress, just notice it and hold it for tomorrow. Each new moment is a new opportunity to Level Up. The only Power in the Past is what it shows us for our Next Steps Forward.

Note: Plan for Morning Intention Setting and Evening Reflection regularly going forward as part of your Mindset in Motion practice.

<u>Day Six- Mindset Journal Activity</u>:

Setting Daily Intentions

After your Mindset affirmation exercise, complete these
statements:

Today, I will Purpose myself to...

____

____

____

____

The Promises that I make to myself today are...

____

____

____

____

The Intentions that I choose to set in motion for today are…

____

____

____

____

At the conclusion of the day, be accountable to yourself by reflecting on how well you held to the promises you made to yourself.

The Promises and Intentions that I kept for myself today are…

____

____

____

____

**The Intentions that I will set for myself tomorrow
are…**

____

____

____

____

Additional Thoughts, Awareness, Challenges for
Part One- Getting Ready for Change:

____

____

____

____

____

____

____

____

____

____

space for reflection

part two:

Awareness Into Action

Staying In Motion ▶

day seven
"Establishing Your Anchors"

Daily Morning Practice: Set your Morning Intentions for Optimizing Your Day

Finding Your Positive Vibe ▶

An Anchor, by Wikipedia standards, is "A device, normally made of metal, used to secure a vessel to the bed of a body of water to prevent the craft from drifting due to wind or current." In our own cultural understanding of the word Anchor, we know it to be something that we use to keep us steady, when otherwise the winds and current might take us places that we do not wish to be. The metaphor of an Anchor is significant in Mindset work. An Anchor, when related to mindset, is any thought, feeling, or sensation that "keeps us steady" in the "winds or currents of change, challenge, stress, grief, or even just regular hecticness". We will use them quite often, and with pleasure. Anchors are the place of solace in our minds, that we will learn how to access anytime, anywhere. Today, the only job is to figure out what they are. Your Anchors will be unique to you and your life experiences.

Have you ever been driving along and a song comes on the stereo that immediately sends a rush of that Feel-Good feeling through you? Though your eyes are still fixed on the streets, signs, and cars in front of you, you can actually see a picture of a time before in your "mind's eye" related to that song. It might be of an old boyfriend or girlfriend, a childhood friend, or a special vacation or holiday. Suddenly, you can't stop yourself from smiling (inside and out). This experience of the past has left an imprint in your mind's neural network, and it exists in that network- sometimes active, sometimes dormant. It may fade or get fuzzy over time, but it is there. And all it takes is that one song to make it active again. Through the sense of sound, this song becomes an association to a variety of other senses that are 'wired in' to your mind's perceptive reality, and therefore, memory. So not only does the song bring with it the sensation of a delightful sound, but it also elicits images, maybe smells or tastes even, and most certainly feelings in both physicality and emotion. It also has the potential to reconnect to a previous state of being, idea, or belief about oneself, the world, or life in general. Think about it: a song that reminds you of a happy memory in your life likely also transports you to the quality of life of that time, and the schemas that you possessed there, such as: the innocence of childhood, the optimism that the world was for your taking and that anything was possible, the hopefulness of true love, and so on.

That means that tapping into one network imprint can bring forth sensations, feelings, thoughts, and even beliefs that once served you and can serve you again. Your Mindset Anchors may have attachments to people, places, and things, but the experience of them lives inside of you, which means you can access when you so desire. Summing it up, this experience is anchored to a particular feeling that resides within you as sensory memory. Attached to it are certain thoughts and even beliefs that are aligned with the feeling it produces. This state of being and belief lives inside of your unique reality data bank. You can make a withdrawal from that bank whenever you choose. Going forward, we will practice exactly that. Use <u>Day Seven- Creating an Anchor Journal Activity</u> to designate your personal anchors.

Evening Mindset Practice: Reflect on the Promises that you made to yourself at the start of this day and add at least 1 minute of reflection back to your Anchoring experience in today's Journal Activity.

<u>Day Seven- Mindset Journal Activity</u>:
Creating an Anchor

This exercise, done correctly, will require at least 10 minutes of dedicated time and attention.

It's time to establish some Anchors. Let's a take trip down memory lane to find some! Fill in the information below to identify and develop your personal mindset anchors:

The feeling that I seek most often is

_______________________________________.

The time that I felt this in a profound way was

____

____

____

_______________________________________.

Now, after you have identified the feeling-state you are wanting most, close your eyes, and see yourself in a movie theater. Picture the time you answered above on the screen. Fill in the box on the following page with this memory using words or pictures.

Spend time here in this picture screen/feeling state (5-10 minutes if possible).

What I see, hear, and feel around me in this picture is:

What I see in myself is:

What I hear myself saying is:

The feeling I have inside is:

space for reflection

day eight
"Pause with Purpose"

Daily Morning Practice: Set your Morning Intentions for Optimizing Your Day

It feels so good to give yourself a moment to reconnect with a pleasing memory, feeling, thought, or condition. But it is also important to implement our anchors mindfully. If you are going a million miles a minute in your day and then just decide that at 12:00pm you will find an anchor, you might be frustrated and disappointed when you are not feeling the feeling that you are looking for.

Think of a freight train going down a track at full speed and then the conductor decides to switch tracks- not a smooth transition. Or, when we are driving on the highway at 65 miles an hour, we move over to the right lane, slow down incrementally, and use an indicator as we approach the exit. In the same way, when *we* are about to make a change, we need to move into another lane, put on our turn signal, and slow it down before our anchor can be used most effectively.

Today we will practice The Pause. For those who know Yoga, it will be your mental "Child's Pose" in your practice. A moment to find rest in Body and Mind before continuing on. Be careful though, this is not a mindless "numb out" moment. This is a moment to **Pause with Purpose**.

In addition to today's intentions, plan to schedule three moments of Mindful Pause in the day.

Select a time and set an alarm on your phone or watch if needed. Set yourself up for success. Select times that you have at least a 75% chance that you can mentally and/or physically remove yourself from "the day" to pause for 3-5 minutes.

When it is time to Pause, find a place to retreat in. This can be an actual physical relocation (i.e., step away from your desk, go outside, go into a restroom stall). Or it can simply be an internal relocation (i.e., STOP working, doing, thinking). When you are there, withdraw from the stimuli of the environment by closing your eyes…

<u>Mindset Practice</u>

Slowing Your Roll ▶

Now Just Breathe.

Notice the breath. Going In; Going Out.

Feel your lungs and belly fill with the air that comes in; Feel the air leaving the belly and lungs as it goes out.

Hear the word "Breathe".

If a thought floats in. Just notice it and allow it to float out with the next exhale.

Be here. In this Moment. Only.

And Breathe.

Let yourself stay in this place for at least 3 minutes if you can. If you can only do 1 minute, that's okay too. This is A Practice; **Perfection does not apply here.**

Use the <u>Day Eight- Mindful Pause Journal Activity</u> to do an inventory of your experience.

Evening Mindset Practice*:* Reflect on how it felt today to Pause and Be Still.

<u>Day Eight- Mindset Journal Activity</u>:

Self-Inventory/Mindful Pause

What did my mindful pausing show me today?

____

____

____

____

What differences did I notice in my mind and in my body when enacting mindful pauses?

____

____

____

____

How did mindful pausing impact my decisions, choices, and actions?

____

____

____

____

How did mindful pausing give me agency over myself today?

____

____

____

____

Were there challenges to remembering and/or achieving mindful pauses today?

81

____

____

____

How might I improve my efforts to pause more mindfully tomorrow?

____

____

____

____

space for reflection

day nine
"Grabbing Hold of Your Anchor"

Daily Morning Practice: Set your Morning Intentions and add one minute of Pause.

Grabbing onto a Good Feeling ▶

The Foundation has been set. You now have your Mindset Anchors ready. And you also have a Mindfulness practice of Pause under your belt. It is time to Use your Anchor.

Continue with the Intentions you set yesterday for three moments of Pause in the day. The day might be different today, so it is not necessary for the times to stay the same. Just make sure there are at least three moments of your choosing. Design the day as you wish and set yourself up for success by selecting the times that will work for you on *this* day or select times that you recognize you need an anchor (i.e.-moments of stress, business, frustration, boredom, etc.).

Either in the last 60 seconds of or following your Pause Time, "Grab onto your Anchor". That means go to the picture on the movie screen you depicted on <u>Day 7</u>. Be there.

Mindset Practice
Push Your Pause Button ▶

See the images. See yourself in this place.

Hear the Sounds. Hear the words you are offering to yourself in this image.

Tune into the overarching beliefs and awareness that you have here.

Feel the sensations that your body feels like in this version of yourself.

Breathe in the internal emotions and feelings in this moment.

Hold onto all of this for 60 seconds (or more).

Note: sometimes an actual visual reminder or tactile tool can be helpful in accessing an anchored sensation/belief/feeling. Use what works!

If you have an object of association to a desired feeling or anchor, bring it with you today. Maybe a picture, a piece of meaningful jewelry, a hand-crafted gift from a loved one. If you can wear it or keep it with you throughout the day, even better. If not, that's okay too. Remember, this experience along with all the associated sensations, feelings, and beliefs already reside within you. You possess all of it. You are not *creating* this feeling. You are simply anchoring on to something that you already have experienced in order to experience it again, in the present moment.

Use the <u>Day Nine-Anchoring Journal Activity</u> on the next page to account for how you used your anchors today.

Evening Mindset Practice: Reflect on the Promises that you made to yourself at the start of this day. At the conclusion, spend at least 1 minute of Pause and 2-3 minutes of Anchoring.

<u>Day Nine- Mindset Journal Activity</u>:

Self-Inventory ABC (Using my Anchors):

Write your answers to the following 'ABC' questions in the
ABC Chart on the following pages.

<u>A (Antecedent/ Time and Situation)</u>:

What was happening right before you used your anchor?

<u>B (Behavior/ Using an Anchor)</u>:

What was your Anchor and how did you use it?

<u>C (Conclusion/ Outcome)</u>:

What did you notice after responding to the antecedent event
by employing an anchor?

A (Antecedent/ Time and Situation):	**B** (Behavior/ Using an Anchor):	**C** (Conclusion/ Outcome):

A (Antecedent/ Time and Situation):	**B** (Behavior/ Using an Anchor):	**C** (Conclusion/ Outcome):

space for reflection

day ten
"Roadblocks"

Daily Morning Practice: Set your Morning Intentions and Anchor to a Safe Place.

Discovering Barriers ▶

So often, when there is a challenge or goal in our lives, we engage thoughts that create barriers to our success. Thoughts like: "What if this doesn't work out?", "What if I *Can't* do it?", "This is so hard.", etc.

These thoughts have only one purpose- to keep you protected from the thing that feels scary: Change. This is what is called resistance, and it usually comes from somewhere and ends up as a repetitious habit in our thinking.

This is not to minimize the concerns, worries, and fears that we have about stepping outside of our comfort zones. It is, however, to be able to recognize that these fears are often based more so in a need to feel safe and protect ourselves from the unknown and potential disappointment, then they are REAL dangers that we are facing. The brain cannot differentiate between Discomfort and Danger unless the Mind consciously gives it allowance to. The brain is wired to have a biological response to anything that it senses to be a danger. The Mind houses a collection of information, knowledge, experience, and understanding that allows it to make sense of the incoming data and determine whether or not there is a real and imminent danger approaching.

So often, we respond to the discomforts in our life as though they are dangers for this reason. We just go with what the brain is reacting to. When we begin a change process of any kind, it feels really uncomfortable, and it is likely that our brain will react accordingly. It will send us into a type of 'fight or flight' response because this discomfort feels like a danger signal. An inner power struggle can begin to ensue as one part of us wants desperately to make a change, and the other is hunkering down trying to protect itself. Ultimately, we find ourselves stuck between the two. Developing greater mindfulness, present moment awareness, and a broader growth mindset positions us to respond to these mis-signals and inner struggles once we can understand ourselves well enough to know what is happening and figure out how to navigate a path through the roadblock.

Today our focus will be solely on Becoming more Aware of the Roadblocks that we come up against in the process of change. We will pay very close attention to the thoughts going on 'inside your head' that are aligned with this Protection from Change. We are not going to Worry about them; We are just going to become aware of them. Use the <u>Day Ten- Roadblocks Journal Activity</u> to collect the roadblock thoughts and habits that you become aware of throughout the day.

Evening Mindset Practice: Spend 5-10 minutes Visioning. At the conclusion, spend at least 5 minutes in the practice of Pause and Anchor.

<u>Day Ten- Mindset Journal Activity</u>:
Roadblocks

Keep this journal (or loose paper, a notebook, or post-it notes) with you throughout the day. Anytime you notice a thought that sounds like a "What if I can't", or "This is too hard" type of thought, jot it down. When your activities for the day are complete, move onto the second part of today's Journal Activity.

____

____

____

____

____

____

____

____

____

____

____

____

Sit down and collect the Roadblock Thoughts you ran into throughout your day by capturing/re-writing them in the STOP sign below. **Notice any themes as you do.**

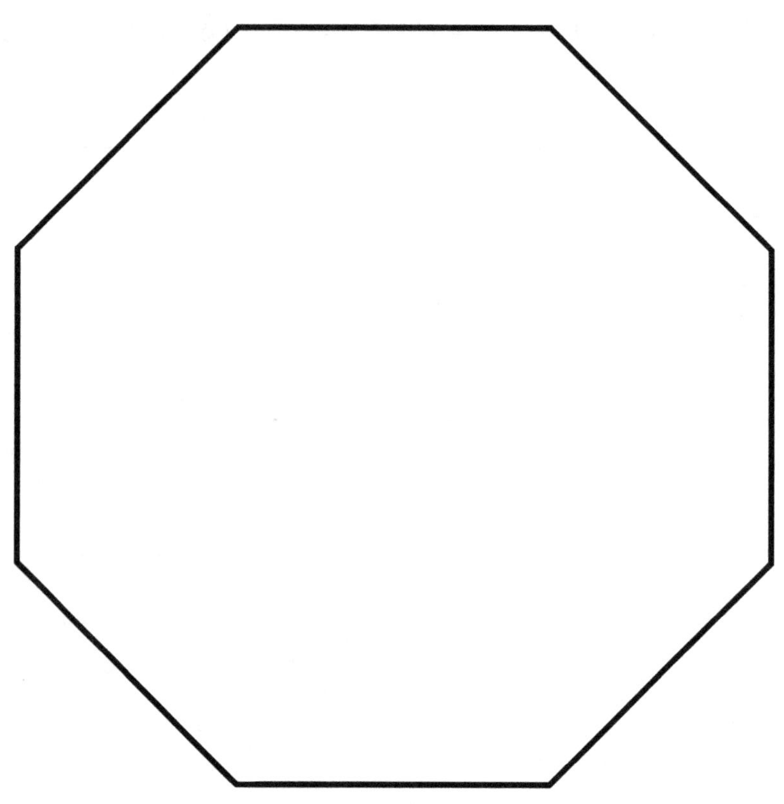

space for reflection

day eleven
"Radical Acceptance"

Daily Morning Practice: Set your Morning Intentions and Anchor to a Safe Place.

The operational definition of Radical Acceptance is "when you stop fighting reality". It does not mean that you agree with the situation or excuse it, you simply get out of the cycle of trying to fight its realness. You meet yourself in the moment that you ARE IN, as opposed to the moment that you think you SHOULD BE IN. In so doing, you are dialing down any voice of judgment or ridicule toward yourself, and positioning yourself more successfully toward making a mindful, non-reactive, non-defensive choice toward the next step.

Our Mindset in Motion journey has now led us up to a place of greater understanding about ourselves and figuring out why we get stuck when we try to affect change in our lives. We have either learned more or at least become more consciously aware of how experiences in our lives have prompted certain protective measures in our thoughts and in behaviors. Those measures helped us in one regard, and we use them over and over for lengths of time and eventually those measures become habits. The purpose of calling this to attention in the change process is Acceptance. Similar to how we accepted our starting point on this change journey back on Day Two, now we are invited to accept *how* we got here.

We will not linger in this space too long, only long enough to achieve a Moment of Radical Acceptance and to get out of any inner power struggles. This gives us a Realness with ourselves that is required for sustainable growth and change.

Use the <u>Day Eleven- Radical Acceptance Journal Activity</u> to identify points of Acceptance about who you are, where you are, and the path that brought you here. *After* completing the Journal Activity, use the following Mindset Practice to rewire how you think about these points of Acceptance.

With Acceptance comes Empowerment.

Mindset Practice

Acceptance Equals Empowerment ▶

Today, reinstate or continue a plan to Pause with Purpose (as you did in Day 8).

In each Pause, do the following:

Pause.

Breathe.

Notice the breath. Going In; Going Out.

Feel your lungs and belly fill with the air that comes in; Feel the air leaving the belly and lungs as it goes out.

Hear yourself say: "I Accept You as You Are in this Moment Right Here and Now, and I Honor the Road that you have traveled to get Here".

Now take a deeper breath with emphasis on the inhale (Breathe this statement into your Being), and slowly exhale to achieve Calm.

Evening Mindset Practice*: Reflect on the Promises you made to yourself today. Spend 5-10 minutes Visioning. At the conclusion, spend at least 5 minutes in the practice of Pause and Anchor.

Day Eleven- Mindset Journal Activity:
Radical Acceptance

Along this path, write down points that you now Accept about Who you are, where you are, and the people, life events, and circumstances that have contributed to getting you Here.

Be sure to Identify ALL aspects of yourself in this Acceptance activity. Include strengths, talents, qualities, along with any areas you may want to change.

space for reflection

day twelve
"Naming Your Needs"

Daily Morning Practice: Set your Morning Intentions and add one minute of Anchoring to a Safe Place.

How Do Your Habits Meet Your Needs? ▶

Our Roadblocks show up originally for a reason, and usually a very good one. Throughout our lives, they have helped us avoid things that felt bad. And while we can usually recognize the roadblock itself pretty easily, the Need behind it can sometimes be elusive to us.

Day Ten's exercise hopefully illuminated the roadblocks that may have been holding you back up until now. Some you may have already been aware of; others may have been a new discovery to you. Bringing our unconscious habits and defense mechanisms into the light, or consciousness, is a great and necessary step at breaking down resistance to change. The next step that will lead us to working through that resistance is understanding what Needs those roadblocks are guarding.

So, now that the roadblocks are named, let's dig deeper into where they come from so that we can determine the needs they are representing.

Today's exercise is intended to further your understanding of yourself, honor the journey that has come before, and continue to answer meaningful questions about what is needed to get out of any "stuck" points. Asking yourself meaningful questions unlocks doors to greater understanding and begins the shift from unconscious reactive decisions to that of Mindful Choices.

Use the <u>Day Twelve- Needs Assessment Journal Activity</u> to prompt your reflection. While today's activity may generate uncomfortable memories from past challenges, remember you are in a safe space now, simply reflecting for the purpose of gathering information that will help you grow. If needed, use your anchors to help you stay grounded in the present moment and focused on your positive path of change to find balance should any areas of discomfort arise. This activity is not for the purpose of "unpacking old stuff". It is simply to identify and honor any unmet needs from past experiences that might be influencing your roadblocks today.

Evening Mindset Practice: Spend 5-10 minutes Visioning. At the conclusion, spend at least 5 minutes in the practice of Pause and Anchor.

<u>Day Twelve- Mindset Journal Activity</u>:

Naming Our Needs

Look back at the 'Roadblock Thoughts' you wrote in your notes on Day 10. Think about the questions below and respond to the following prompts for each Roadblock Thought that you have identified:

What was the first time, or most profound time, that you can recall thinking this Roadblock Thought? How old were you? What was the situation then? What did you need at that time?

Roadblock Thought:

____

____

What did you need at that time?

____

____

What do you need now?

____

____

Roadblock Thought:

____

____

What did you need at that time?

____

____

What do you need now?

____

____

Roadblock Thought:

____

____

What did you need at that time?

____

____

What do you need now?

____

____

Roadblock Thought:

____

What did you need at that time?

____

____

What do you need now?

____

____

Roadblock Thought:

____

____

What did you need at that time?

____

____

What do you need now?

____

____

Roadblock Thought:

____

____

What did you need at that time?

____

____

What do you need now?

____

____

space for reflection

day thirteen
"Self-Compassion"

Daily Morning Practice: Morning Intention Setting & Anchoring

Growth Through Understanding ▶

We hear the term Self-Compassion quite often, but rarely do we really "get" what it means. It can sound like a "feel-good" statement with no substance when we apply it as "giving myself a break" or "not being too hard on myself". For our purposes in this Mindset journal, we will be defining Self-Compassion (operationally) as: a "<u>place where I validate what I need and allow myself to get those needs met</u>".

In order to change habitual thoughts and behaviors we must meet the original Need that was never met in the first place. We can't go back in time to give our 'old' self the reassurance, strength, confidence, and safety that we needed in those past moments. So, instead, we will focus our energy on meeting the needs of our "Here and Now" Self instead.

How many times have you set out on a personal growth goal, gotten sabotaged, and then ridiculed yourself for the failure? This is where we start to feel stuck, and this is where we might start to get down on ourselves and discouraged with the process. Here is where we self-judge, criticize, blame, and put ourselves down. Sometimes we might try to use this negative self-talk for motivation to "try harder". I, personally, have never witnessed that to be successful. For most people, this type of critical self-talk just gets them further down into the stuck place, feeling hopeless and depressed about it. Today, we change that for good!

Think of the example of scolding a child to get a better test grade. How will that child feel in response to that scolding? Will anything said during the scolding assist the child to feel smarter or more capable of getting a better grade? Will any part of hearing words of ridicule motivate them or make them feel confident enough to succeed?... Not likely. Those harsh words will mostly only cause them to feel like a "failure", put pressure on them that will work against their potential, and may even convince them to stop trying because it's 'safer' than the disappointment of future failure.

A Change Mindset is about loving yourself just as you are AND enough to have more, to do more, and to be more! And you cannot achieve that when you are beating yourself up all along the way. More effective is the step process of Acceptance, Compassion, and Nurture. The next few days are going to be focused on this type of Self-Care. This is not the same thing as giving yourself an "excuse" to continue to choose thoughts and actions that do not serve you any longer. That actually sends the opposite message of what we want here by suggesting that you are not capable of more. This is simply replacing the moment of judgment with a moment of acceptance in your own head. And from there, a next step toward meeting the need at hand so that you can keep going forward and leaning in a new direction. Use the <u>Day Thirteen- Self-Compassion Mindset Journal Activity</u> to begin this new conversation with yourself.

Evening Mindset Practice: Read ahead to tomorrow's Activity so that you can begin to plan for the day. If your schedule tomorrow does not allow for you to enact a Self-Care plan, pause the journey here, and schedule that self-care day within 3 days' time, and then resume.

Day Thirteen- Mindset Journal Activity:

Self-Compassion

Look back at your <u>Day Twelve- Naming Your Needs Journal Activity</u> and reflect on the Needs you wrote down in each Roadblock situation. Use the prompts on the following pages to practice meeting those needs with a statement of Self-Compassion that will aid in meeting the Needs of the past and present.

Either carry this journal with you or write down your Statements of Self-Compassion on something you can carry with you all day long (post-its, index cards, notes on your phone, etc.). Anytime you find yourself in a Roadblock Moment, read to yourself (either inside or out loud) the statements that correspond with the voice in your head. Over and Over... All day long, as many times as you need to.

Example:

<u>Roadblock</u>*- Fear of failure*

<u>Need</u>*- Reassurance and safety*

<u>Statement of Self Compassion</u>*- It's understandable to be afraid. Remember that you are capable of handling this change, and you are going to be OKAY!*

Roadblock:

____

Need(s):

____

Statement of Self Compassion:

____

____

Roadblock:

____

Need(s):

____

Statement of Self Compassion:

____

____

Roadblock:

____

Need(s):

____

Statement of Self Compassion:

____

____

Roadblock:

____

Need(s):

____

Statement of Self Compassion:

____

____

Roadblock:

____

Need(s):

____

Statement of Self Compassion:

____

____

Roadblock:

____

Need(s):

____

Statement of Self Compassion:

____

____

space for reflection

day fourteen
"Self-Nurture"

Daily Morning Practice: Morning Intentions for Self-Care

The Definition of Nurture:

Verb: "to care for and encourage the growth and development of"

Noun: "the process of caring for and encouraging the growth or development of someone or something"

-*Definition from Oxford Languages*

The concept of nurture usually gets associated with children being mothered or taken care of by their parents. What gets lost is that nurture is not just about "taking care of someone"; it is caring for someone for the encouragement of **growth** and **development**. There is no more perfect way to conceptualize this Mindset Journey that you have embarked on.

Today, there is only one task at hand: *Nurture Yourself.*

Spoil Yourself ▸

Today you will give yourself permission to be Nurtured… by Yourself.

Reflect on the past few days and see if there are any themes that begin to jump out at you.

What do you need most in your day-to-day?

Do you need time? Do you need space?

Do you need safety? Do you need connection?

Do you need comfort? Do you need strength?

Do you need rest? Do you need activity?

The list of needs we may encounter is limitless. Which ones stand out to you the most?

Today you are going to take some time out to create and enact a Self-Care plan with the purpose of meeting those needs.

Use the <u>Day Fourteen- Self-Nurture Journal Activity</u> to create a Self-Care plan that will meet those needs. Think about and enact the answers to the journal questions. Hold yourself accountable to your plan by using the free-write for Reflection on your experience.

Note: Remind yourself that this is a valuable exercise and worth taking the time to do. Do not shrug it off! Only through Acceptance of where you are, what you need, and permitting Yourself to nurture yourself and meet that need will you be able to really move through stuck points in your mind and in your life. This process is essential to your growth and development. If you do not nurture yourself, you stay in the never-ending mindset power struggle that holds you back from sustainable and lasting change.

Evening Mindset Practice: Reflect on how it feels to be in this space of Nurture and Growth; conclude with 2-5 minutes of Anchoring practice.

<u>Day Fourteen- Mindset Journal Activity</u>:

Self-Nurture

Think about the needs you have reflected on and complete the following:

The Needs I will meet for myself today are:

____

____

____

I will meet these Needs by:

____

____

____

What will be required?

(i.e., resources, setting aside time, support from others, etc.):

____

____

____

What Boundaries do I need to set to ensure that I will do what I need?:

With Myself: ___________________________________

____

____

____

With Others: ___________________________________

____

____

____

<u>Reflection</u>: At the conclusion of this day, use this free-write section to reflect on your Day of Self-Nurture. Describe your experience and make note of what you gained, as well as, if there was anything that seemed to get in the way of keeping your Self- Care promises to yourself.

____

____

space for reflection

day fifteen
"Navigation Assistance"

Daily Morning Practice: Set your Morning Intentions and Anchor to a safe place.

Using Your Internal GPS ▶

So far in this journal we have spent considerable time naming our Roadblocks, the Needs that are behind the roadblocks, and practicing methods that will help us meet the needs that the roadblock is trying to protect. Now, that we have improved our awareness, established security, and developed strategies to set us up for success for any roadblocks that might show up, it is time to <u>GO forward</u>.

Pretend you are on a trip and driving down the road with an idea in your mind of where you are headed. Then, suddenly, there is an unexpected roadblock that seems to be keeping you from your destination. Maybe it is a Road Closed sign, or a fallen tree trunk laying across the road. What do you do? Do you stay there in Park waiting for it to go away? Do you quit, turn around, and go back home? Or do you seek out some type of re-navigation assistance. Most likely, and hopefully, it is the latter. But before you can re-navigate, it is important to figure out *how* before you go on. Is there Detour signage that I can look for? Will you use Google, Waze, or Garmin to see the best new route? You quickly assess or reassess where you are, where you are still trying to get to, and what you Need to assist you in getting there. Yet another great metaphor for what the process will look like when we are navigating around or through our own internal roadblocks that makes change feel hard sometimes. We have spent so much time on these roadblocks because these are the moments, reactions, compulsive actions, and unconscious choices that keep us stuck and cause us to self-sabotage. And as we have talked about, these roadblocks are the culprit of that START-STOP-START AGAIN hamster wheel we can find ourselves on.

Herein lies the endless loop of the inner power struggle we all know too well. It's time that we help ourselves out of this viscous cycle. And so, today we are going to use a different approach to this inner conflict and place of impasse. You now know what your roadblocks are. You understand the underlying needs that you are seeking to be met when you are in a roadblock moment. Now, it is time to **APPLY** this knowledge and **RESPOND** to your roadblock moments and situations by meeting the needs of causation and taking your next steps forward.

Use the <u>Day Fifteen- Navigating through Roadblocks Journal Activity</u> to break it down into 3 steps: Roadblock, Needs, and Response.

Evening Mindset Practice: Spend 5-10 minutes Visioning. At the conclusion, spend at least 5 minutes in the practice of Pause and Anchor.

<u>Day Fifteen-Mindset Journal Activity</u>:
Navigating Through Roadblocks

Today, the only questions we are going to ask ourselves in the face of a roadblock are, "What do I need here?" and "How will I meet that Need for myself so that I *can* take the next steps forward?"

Use the information you have collected about and for yourself in <u>Days Ten</u> and <u>Eleven</u> to the complete the 3-step chart on the following pages.

Roadblock (Thought, Feeling, or Behavior)	What are the Needs causing this Roadblock?	What are my next steps to meet the Need and keep going?

Roadblock (Thought, Feeling, or Behavior)	What are the Needs causing this Roadblock?	What are my next steps to meet the Need and keep going?

space for reflection

day sixteen

"Stretching the Norm"

Daily Morning Practice: Set your morning intentions and at the same time, let yourself stretch into the day. Notice any tight spots in your body and in your muscles. Just notice them and offer yourself a gentle stretch in that area while you thoughtfully connect with your intentions for the day.

Staying with the Stretch ▶

Ever watch a dog or a cat move from rest to action? Before they go, they stretch. Instinctively, animals may still know something humans forgot. You need to Stretch yourself before you Move yourself.

Now, you are Present, you are Aware, you are Accepting, you are Anchored, you are Nurtured. You have everything you need at your core foundation, and it is time to Grow. Change and Growth can often be uncomfortable. The term "growing pains" is not a joke.

Remember those aches in the body, and specifically limbs, as a preteen or teenager when your body was doing its job to stretch you taller? This was a time when all the initial, necessary development and nutritional and biological foundation of childhood had prepared you for the expansion of adolescence.

Yes, growth can be uncomfortable, but it is also necessary to thrive! When you have established what you need to get ready for growth it can flourish, and you can tolerate the discomfort with the knowledge of your safety and its value. This is called *Distress Tolerance*.

Today the focus will be on starting to stretch your norms that no longer serve you. It will be like taking a stiff or tight muscle and slowly stretching it so it can become more functional to the rest of your body. This stretch exercise might be uncomfortable at first; that is understandable. It has been stiffened this way for a long time. But you don't quit the stretch because even though it *feels* painful, you **KNOW** that it is necessary to keep stretching to get to a place where it will feel better.

This metaphor applies also to the Habits (of thought and behavior) that you have recognized are your "stiff muscles" in your life. The ones that get in your way of really being able to move and grow. The ones that need to be stretched and worked out.

Today, use <u>Day Sixteen's Stretching the Norm Journal Activity</u> to think about and practice how you are going to Stretch into new areas and new habits in your life.

153

Evening Mindset Practice: Reflect on "Successful Stretches" and spend 5-10 minutes in Visioning practice.

Note: You may want to set aside an extra 10-15 minutes after your Morning Intentions tomorrow to complete Day Seventeen's coursework and journal activity.

<u>Day Sixteen-Mindset Journal Activity</u>:

Stretching the Norm

AWARENESS:

List 1-3 Habits of thought and/or behavior that no longer
serve you on your path toward the Change:

____

____

____

____

____

____

Turn page to take the next Action Step.

ACTION:

Watch out for any of these habits above to present themselves during this day.

When one occurs, respond to it with the following practice:

<u>Distress Tolerance Practice to Break Old Habits:</u>

Pause with Purpose.

Recognize the habit, impulse, thought, or behavior as if it were a "stiff muscle" and…. Breathe.

Observe it but Do Not Engage it and… Breathe.

Allow yourself to Stay with the discomfort that comes from Stretching yourself beyond this habitual stuck point and… Breathe.

Identify if there is anything you Need to be able to maintain the stretch and tolerate the discomfort (i.e. a redirecting or reassuring thought, finding an anchor, a replacement behavior, or even external support that accesses what you need in this moment).

Stay with the Stretch!

Congratulate yourself for stretching past your norm to a new experience.

space for reflection

day seventeen
"Advanced Action Thinking"

Daily Morning Practice: Set your Morning Intentions for Optimizing Your Day

"You have to see it to believe it." Today, we apply this concept by letting ourselves See the change we want in our mind before we try to execute it with our choices and actions.

Let's pull out that Road Map again. Earlier in this journal, we used the idea of a road map to establish the "You are Here" point, and to set incremental and attainable next steps for your journey. Now, having set your itinerary, fueled up, adjusted the rearview mirrors, checked the brakes, and buckled up, you are ready to get on the road. Furthering that metaphor, think about any road trip that you have taken before. When you get in the car and turn on the engine, you have a mental vision of what the day ahead will look like. You might have images of the roads that you anticipate traveling. You might "see" potential traffic or clear roads in your mind's eye as you think about what is ahead of you. You may check online for interesting stops or yummy eateries along the way. Though you may not even be conscious that you are doing it, you are rehearsing for the road ahead. You are imagining what it will look, sound, feel, and even taste like well before you are there in real time.

We might be more aware of how we mentally rehearse things we don't want, which is called worry. When we worry, we anticipate problems in an attempt to prevent or control the variables that might deter what we really want. Most of us have that skill pretty well-honed. So, to borrow something that we already know how to do well, we are simply going to take that skill and turn it around to focus on only positive outcomes.

Today in this Mindset process, we are going to rehearse how we DO want things to go, which is what we will refer to as *Advanced Action Thinking*. Similar to rehearsing for a play, you practice the performance that you want to give BEFORE you are on the stage. This allows us to forge new neural pathways and wire into our minds more data around what we want, instead of staying stuck in a neural rut about more of what we don't want.

Think of this as taking your daily intention setting to the Next Level by rehearsing, and then acting out, your Intentions in very specific ways. Use <u>Day Seventeen-Advanced Action Thinking Journal Activity</u> to mentally practice the thing(s) that you will be thinking, doing, and feeling before they happen. Reflect back to <u>Days Three</u> and <u>Four</u> when you identified your first Next Steps toward change and then imagined what that will look like, sound like, and feel like. Now you get to rehearse the details and make it happen!

Evening Mindset Practice: Reflect on the new habits that you began today and spend 5-10 minutes in Visioning practice.

<u>**Day Seventeen-Journal Activity**</u>:
Advanced Action Thinking

Rehearse the Road Ahead ▶

Select a time today to dedicate at least 10 minutes to your rehearsal. Morning is preferable but you know yourself best, so pick the segment that will work best for you for your best outcome. Give yourself permission to extend this exercise into the next day if needed. When it is time to mentally rehearse, close your eyes, and let your senses show you the way.

<u>Be Specific</u>!

SEE yourself doing the action steps (i.e., organizing your space in a specific way, creating a morning or evening routine, exercising at a specific time, preparing and eating a healthy meal, crushing that presentation at work, reaching out to someone socially, and so on).

HEAR the motivating internal dialogue that you will attach to each action.

FEEL how it will Feel to Do the things that are aligned with your greater/ ideal self.

NOW, use the Cheat Sheet on the following pages to write down your Advanced Action Thoughts in order to bring your Rehearsal to Reality.

<u>**AAT Cheat Sheet:**</u>

On this and the following page, write what you see, hear, and feel in your mental rehearsal. You can also add any other senses that you anticipate (smells or tastes).

Refer to these notes as a reminder (or "cheat sheet for change") throughout the rest of the day.

Today I will:

____

____

____

____

Describe what this looks like in your mind:

____

____

____

____

Describe what you want to hear, both around in and in your own mind *(i.e., your thoughts):*

____

____

____

____

Describe what you want to feel (and any other sensations) in this new situation:

____

____

____

____

Now, use this Cheat Sheet to Make it Happen!

space for reflection

day eighteen
"Shifting into New Beliefs"

Daily Morning Practice: Set your Morning Intentions for the Day and close your practice with this mantra: "I Believe in My Ability to Grow"

Leaning into a Growth Mindset ▶

A **Fixed Mindset** protects us from stepping into areas that feel unknown and scary. If our mind tells us that something must be one way or the other, or all or nothing, we are more inclined to stay where we are to avoid pain, disappointment, and failure.

A **Growth Mindset** empowers us to expand, as we consider all the possibilities as well as the "possibility of new possibility". The potential is endless. If we partner our Self Belief with a Growth Mindset, our personal growth potential becomes endless as well.

As it was stated before in this Mindset Journey, sometimes the jump feels too big to get from here to there. This is the same in our own Self-Belief system. But again, it shouldn't be All or Nothing. If you try to jump from "I CAN'T do anything" to "I CAN do everything" you will likely fall into the chasm between these two points of extreme.

True and honest Self-Belief and Empowerment is not about selling yourself on things that you might reject. It is not about having all the confidence, and all the success, and all of the answers to obliterate natural and habitual doubt. It is about recognizing the doubt yet believing enough in yourself to know you will be able to figure it out, and that you will be able to handle the ride while getting there. The past 17 days have incrementally introduced you to this very thing. Now it is time to integrate and incorporate your mindset practices into what you Believe about yourself.

For sustainable change in Self-Belief, we need to create distance from any fixed ideas that we might have about ourselves and *lean into* any and all ideas that suggest possibility.

Replacing thoughts such as, "I can't" with "I believe that I am capable of learning change", or "I'll *never* be able to" with "I will figure out *how* to".

When you move from fixed to growth mindset thinking, you shift gears, and you Move. Many times, this shift can be just in the way you are thinking about something, and suddenly you liberate yourself to look for solutions instead of problems. In Mindset Work, it is the difference between being stuck and being able. Use <u>Day Eighteen- Shifting Beliefs Journal Activity</u> to make a shift from any fixed mindset beliefs to new growth mindset beliefs.

Evening Mindset Practice: Reflect on any areas of Growth you have noticed in your habits, your routines, your thoughts, and your choices during this Mindset Journey. Honor Your Progress by listing your gratitudes for who you are today, and what potential you have for tomorrow.

<u>Day Eighteen-Journal Activity</u>:

Shifting Beliefs

During the past 17 days you have shown yourself your potential for Change. You will now use that new evidence of your potential to shift your Self-Belief statements toward Self-Empowerment.

Reflect on any former and/or still present Fixed Mindset Self-Beliefs and write them in the left column.

Respond to each with a Shifting Statement that reflects your new Growth Mindset and Empowers you to believe in your potential for growth in that area. Write that Self-Empowerment Statement in the respective right column.

Fixed Mindset Self-Belief:	Growth Mindset Self-Belief:

Fixed Mindset Self-Belief:	Growth Mindset Self-Belief:

space for reflection

day nineteen:
"Designing Your Day"

Daily Morning Practice: Set your Morning Intentions for the Day, close your practice by adding this mantra:

"I AM Capable of the Change I want for myself, I HAVE What I Need to make that change happen, and I CAN DO what I set out to do."

Make it Your Own ▶

Resiliency theory has taught us that in order to be resilient, we need to be able to have positive thoughts about the following prompts:

I Have _____________, I Can _____________, I AM _____________.

Beyond being resilient, positive HAVE, CAN, AM thoughts are also the backbone of CHANGE.

When we can say and believe that we HAVE the potential and the internal resources necessary for change, and that we CAN be successful in the changes we seek to achieve, and that we ARE a complete and loveable being all along the way, then we do not fear change itself.

This Mindset Journey has invited you to evaluate yourself, accept yourself as you are and where you are, embrace and meet your intrapersonal needs, stretch and expand toward personal growth, build distress tolerance within the growing pains of that expansion, try on new thoughts and behaviors, and believe in yourself enough to see it through. Throughout these practices, you have gathered new awareness and new evidence that today's morning mantra is true. It is time to take ownership of this self-narrative that you are worthy and capable of getting what you want.

Today is about pulling it all together and applying your newly acquired Mindset concepts and tools freely and actively throughout your day to make it your own.

Look back on the exercises and activities throughout this course and pick out the ones that meant the most to you. Then, put your New Awareness into New Action by using the steps in the <u>Day Nineteen-Making It Yours Journal Activity</u> to reinforce your new narrative, design your own mindset practice, and create a plan for how you will apply it in your day.

Remember to continue to show yourself evidence that You *Have* what you need to keep it going, that You *Can* set intentions and keep your promises to yourself, and that you *Are* Worthy of achieving what you desire.

Evening Mindset Practice: Reflect on the promises that you made and kept to yourself today. Take 5-10 minutes to create the Vision for tomorrow. Within that Vision for tomorrow, rehearse what, when, and how you will keep tomorrow's promises.

<u>Day Nineteen-Journal Activity</u>:

Your Day by Design

Step 1: Fill in each prompt with a positive statement

My New Narrative is:

I Have ____,

I Can ____,

I AM ____.

Step 2: Identify one Mindfulness and/or Mindset practice that you liked the most, was the most enlightening or meaningful, or just made you feel good. It's yours now! Feel free to make it your own in any way that feels right to you.

<u>My New Mindset Practice is:</u>

____

____

Step 3: Create Your Plan. Map out a plan for when you will apply this practice in your day. Complete the following promises you will make to yourself for this practice. Provide the details of when and how you plan to apply/ execute your practice, and a statement about the reason why this practice is important to you or why you deserve to make this a priority.

<u>My New Plan is:</u>

I will use this practice ________________________________,
(WHEN)

by ____,
(HOW)

because ____.
(WHY)

(Use the following prompts for any additional mindset practices that you want to apply to your day)

I will use this practice ________________________________,
(WHEN)

by ____,
(HOW)

because ____.
(WHY)

I will use this practice ___________________________,
(WHEN)

by _________________________________,
(HOW)

because ________________________________.
(WHY)

I will use this practice ___________________________,
(WHEN)

by _________________________________,
(HOW)

because ________________________________.
(WHY)

space for reflection

self-worth

I wanted to share an extra note about something that I think is one of the biggest roadblocks many of us can face. I know, for me, recognizing my self-worth and creating a new narrative that reminds me of my self-worth has had a profound impact on my Mindset Journey.

When we are young, we receive so many messages about who we are and what we deserve. We might find ourselves even subscribing to the "haves" and "have-nots" cast cultures of the world. We eventually internalize these outside sources of scrutiny and they become Inside Voices that lead us to self-beliefs that we are just not good enough, not deserving enough, and not worthy of getting the "good stuff" that this life has to offer. These beliefs and identity blueprints can also be handed down to us from generation to generation as a result of hardships of the past.

And while we should not minimize the struggles and challenges that we have faced, or those of others before us, it is necessary to find a way to not give that history the power to create a present narrative that suggests we lack the worth to have more.

A major part of creating a Mindset that supports the path you are taking to affect change is letting the voice inside your head tell you that you are Worthy of that change. Hopefully there are or have been people in your life to send you this message. If not, I want you to know that you ARE Worthy of succeeding and attaining your goals. Whether you have been told this by others, or you are just hearing it here for the first time, it will only matter to you if you allow it in. Your knowledge of Self-Worth must begin and end with YOU. A belief is simply a thought that you keep thinking. The only way to change a belief is to practice thinking new thoughts.

So, to help you with this, I am sharing my personal practice that has helped me to shift my personal narrative into one that recognizes that I am "Worthy" of chasing my dreams, reaching my goals, and receiving the Abundance that the Universe has for me. Remember our old blueprint is wired in pretty well, so prepare to use this as a PRACTICE (which means just doing it one or two times won't be enough). Make this a new part of everyday so that you can activate a new neural path toward a new self-narrative.

<u>*Self-Worth Practice*</u>

Step into Your Self-Worth ▶

Use the following metaphor to practice thoughts of Self-Worth:

The plants of the earth never shy away from the rays of the sun. They never reduce themselves to block off the goodness of the abundant light. They count themselves worthy of absorbing this source of life to thrive.

Allow yourself a moment each morning before you enter into your day to step into this metaphor.

Be the plant by opening yourself up to the "good stuff" that is coming your way so that you too can thrive.

Let in opportunity, Let in possibility, Let in your own potential, and hear yourself saying repeatedly:

"You are worthy of the good things to come."

space for reflection

the end is the beginning

…And the Journey Never Ends ▶

My Wish for You–

It is my sincere hope that this Mindset Journey has been a positive experience for you. This journey was intended to be a companion's guide along your own personal journey of life and transformation. You are the explorer on your own expedition. Hopefully, this 19-day journey can provide a part of the map to get there.

As I said at the beginning, Mindset is Everything. Whatever your desires are; whatever your goals in life are, knowing how to take ownership and work with your Mindset will determine your success. Tapping into that Power that lives within You is transformative. This Change begins from Within, and then it expands and grows into our outside world and into becoming our new reality. This is Real Change; This is Lasting Change.

If we come at it from any other way, there's a good chance it just won't stick.

My Hope for You is that you know that you are Worthy of whatever you seek, that you Accept yourself as you are, and Love yourself enough to give yourself permission to have More (if that's what you want). I hope, in some small way, this journey has shown you the direction to get there. This journey was about getting your Mindset in Motion, but this is not the end because Yours continues. Take these practices and Go Explore! There is no limit to what you can DO, HAVE, and BE!

Enjoy the Journey!

Wishing You Wellness of Mind and Abundance in Life,

JSK

space for reflection

acknowledgments

*A special thank you
to my editor, creative companion, wordsmith partner,
and right-hand woman, Katelyn Gore.
For without whom, all the ideas in my head would never
get to breathe life.*

about the author

As a Licensed Professional Counselor and Board-Certified Life Coach, Jen Krencicki has been in the field of mind health and personal development for over 25 years. She has experience working as a multi-faceted professional with children, adolescents, adults, couples, and families. Her attention is on promoting mindfulness and mindset strategies to shift thoughts and perspectives that support well-being and self-actualization. Her intent is to make these practices accessible to anyone wanting a mindset shift on life's challenges and important matters.

As a therapist, mindfulness teacher, and mindset coach, she utilizes awareness building, action planning, and the power of possibility to partner with others as they purpose themselves to find their own unique personal life balance of **mind, body, and spirit.**

Jen's academic training began with a BA in Art Therapy & Psychology from Trenton State College, then earning her Masters of Science in Counseling & Human Relations at Villanova University. She studied under the Institute of Life Coach Training and earned her Board Certification as a life coach in 2017, and her Mindfulness Teacher Certification in 2023 through the Mindfulness Certification Training program.